RASPBERRY PI 3:2016 USER GUIDE FOR BEGINNERS

Thomas Charleston

Disclaimer and Terms of Use:

Effort has been made to ensure that the information in this book is accurate and complete, however, the author and the publisher do not warrant the accuracy of the information, text and graphics contained within the book due to the rapidly changing nature of science, research, known and unknown facts and internet. The Author and the publisher do not hold any responsibility for errors, omissions or contrary interpretation of the subject matter herein. This book is presented solely for motivational and informational purposes only.

Contents

CHAPTER 1:
THE RISE OF THE RASPBERRY DYNASTY

I bet if someone had told you that a computer as tiny and shaped like a regular credit in your wallet is soon to storm the market in the nearest future, you would take the person for a joke. But today, that joke has become a reality.

The year 2012 in its prime, witnessed the birth of yet another technological wonder. What makes this more significant is because it was least expected. The world had its eye at that time for smartphones and hybrid gadgets, but not a macro-central processing unit. Hence, the crazy and light it attracted to itself. Since its launch in 2012 the Pi has exceeded expectations, becoming a must-have piece of computer hardware for enthusiasts and tech-heads. For a small project developed to be sold to schools and colleges to teach programming principles, that's not so bad.

Perhaps you are yet to explore the world of the raspberry, which I can tell you is the trendy thing in the world of technology. The emergency of the raspberry and what it has become today remains a marvel to the technologist and the world at large. No one would have thought that a tiny chip, the size of a credit card could be programmed into a computer. Still in doubt, maybe you should purchase a copy yourself and behold its wonder.

The Raspberry Pi is a series of credit card-sized single-board computers developed in the United Kingdom by the Raspberry Pi Foundation to promote the teaching of basic computer science in schools and developing countries. The original Raspberry Pi and Raspberry Pi 2 are manufactured in several board configurations through licensed manufacturing agreements with Newark element14 (Premier Farnell), RS Components and Egoman. The hardware is the same across all manufacturers. The firmware is closed-source.

Several generations of Raspberry Pi's have been released. The first generation (Pi 1) was released in February 2012 in basic model A and a higher specification model B. A+ and B+ models were released a year later. Raspberry Pi 2 model B was released in February 2015 and Raspberry Pi 3 model B in February 2016. These boards are priced between 20 and 35 US$. A cut down "compute" model was released in April 2014, and a Pi Zero with smaller size and limited input/output (I/O), general-purpose input/output (GPIO), abilities released in November 2015 for 5 US$.

All models feature a Broadcom system on a chip (SoC), which includes an ARM compatible central processing unit (CPU) and an on chip graphics processing unit (GPU, a VideoCore IV). CPU speed ranges from 700 MHz to 1.2 GHz for the Pi 3, and on board memory ranges from 256 MB to 1 GB RAM. Secure Digital SD cards are used to store the operating system and program memory in either the SDHC or MicroSDHC sizes. Most boards have between one and four USB slots, HDMI and composite video output, and a 3.5 mm phono jack for audio. The lower level output is provided by a number of GPIO pins which support common protocols like I2C. Some models have an 8P8C Ethernet port and the Pi 3 has on board Wi-Fi 802.11n and Bluetooth.

The Foundation provides Debian and Arch Linux ARM distributions for download, and promotes Python as the main programming language, with support for BBC BASIC (via the RISC OS image or the Brandy Basic clone for Linux), C, C++, PHP, Java, Perl, Ruby, Squeak Smalltalk, and more also available.

However, from its inception till now, the raspberry continues to rise in popularity. Recently, the US government considered purchasing the raspberry as learning tools for schools.

In February 2016, the Raspberry Pi Foundation announced that they had sold eight million devices, making it the best-selling UK personal computer, ahead of the Amstrad PCW.

Have you recently purchased the latest series of the Raspberry, the Raspberry Pi 3? Wondering what features it possess? Or pondering how to best maximize the device? Then sit back, relax and allow us to take you on a tour of the latest device yet in the series of the Raspberry.

CHAPTER 2:
UNBOXING OF THE RASPBERRY
Pi 3

Away from the fact that the Raspberry is a unique and advanced type of the Raspberry family, one must be aware of the fact that four years was put into work before this wonder could be forged.

The main focus of the Raspberry Pi 3 is "connectivity". The wireless and the Bluetooth feature is the one highly anticipated feature of the Raspberry. With this resolved in the Pi 3, it automatically opens up the apparent limited market of the Raspberry.

The Raspberry Pi 3 like its predecessors follows the same pattern; slim, sleek, credit=card shaped, transparent casing, but a quite different specification. Perhaps, like any other technological piece that receives an upgrade, it is always expected that an upgrade must do better than the first or inaugural creation. With every update comes a mind-blowing feature, something that would propel you to discard the existing one and purchase the new one; raspberry Pi 3 is no different or exception to this rule.

What to expect

Before we begin its formal dissecting, let us unveil what to expect from the box:

- ✓ A box containing the "stuff". Simple as it is, the difference between this covering and its predecessor, is its name and production year, and of course, color.
- ✓ The raspberry itself in a black "over-all"
- ✓ The casing itself is two layered. Still curious? You can remove the first layer.
- ✓ The board itself
- ✓ All mounted, you have a solid Raspberry Pi 3.

The casting itself is solid, it can be dismounted easily and reassembled in the same manner, provided you did not forcefully open it up initially. The top can be taken off to feel the board, connect peripherals to the board, and to allow easy installation of these devices.

Perhaps there is even room provided on the board for the installation of a fan to cool the board and reduce heat. How else could this tiny credit card shaped computer be amazing? The casing won't slide easily when placed on top of a slippery surface due to the rubber at the bottom casing.

Away from all these, when you properly assemble this machine, you notice an improved startup speed - one that supersedes its predecessors.

The notion that the raspberry Pi 3 is born after four long years since the launch of the original Raspberry Pi series, opens our minds to the fact that the latest member of the family passed through a whole lot of examination and checks before birth and this is why the product is successful.

The co-founder of the project, Eben Upton, in an interview commented on the birth of the Raspberry Pi 3; he said that the culmination of the team's ambitions, the Raspberry Pi 3, particularly excites him for one main reason: "Connectivity. The other stuff is just a quantitative change - it is faster; wireless and Bluetooth is the biggest step change on this device."

This was an issue that users had complained about. With the emergence of the Raspberry Pi 3, that is a thing of the past.

The Raspberry Pi 3 comes with an open source license. Enclosed in its board is a 64bit operating system, 1.2GHz processing speed, Bluetooth, and a wireless LAN. The Raspberry Pi 3 is unique in itself with attributes and functions that make it fit to continue the tradition of the Raspberries before it. The main attributes it portrays includes:

- ✓ It is faster. With a 1.2GHz processing speed combined with a 64bit operating system, this is definitely a redefinition of the Raspberry genealogy.
- ✓ It has the exact similarity of the series. As simple as this feature is, and might seem an unnecessary one, you may want to consider this: for existing users of the Raspberry, you need not dispose of your old casing. It will still work.
- ✓ It is wireless. This is one feature that clearly separates the Pi 3 from other series before it. Raspberry users had anticipated this feature before now. Connectivity is one major concern, and can be tagged as the major landmark of the Raspberry Pi 3.

CHAPTER 3:
GETTING ACQUAINTED WITH THE RASPBERRY Pi 3

The Raspberry Pi 3 is an amazing tool that promises to ease work and play. Its distinctive features are far more convincing. The Raspberry Pi 3 is one device that all should get. It is only a matter of time before this wonder replaces the regular desktop in every home. Especially a community that wants to improve learning at a reduced cost. That it is tiny and cheap, makes up for the tendency that the device will be greatly embraced as long as its upgrades continue to satisfy the ever demanding tech users. Below are some basic inclusions on the Broadcom of the Raspberry Pi 3:

- ✓ **Antenna**: This confirms that the Raspberry originators had users of the older series in mind by working on the complaint logged. The antenna being inbuilt, connected and soldered directly to the board resolves the problem of wanting to fix an external antenna thereby expanding the board unnecessarily. The antenna should be capable of picking up wireless LAN, and Bluetooth signals no matter how far regardless of the obstacles in front.

- ✓ **Wireless Radio**: You may want to doubt this feature because it is barely visible on the board. It is small and its markings can be seen properly through a microscope or magnifying glass. The Broadcom BCM43438 chip provides wireless LAN, Bluetooth Classic radio support. Cleverly built directly onto the board to keep cost down, rather than the more common fully qualified module approach, its only unused feature is a disconnected FM radio receiver.

✓ **SoC**: This feature is but distinctive and exclusive for the Raspberry Pi 3. The Broadcom BCM2837 system-on-chip (SoC) includes "four" high-performance ARM Cortex-A53 processing cores running at 1.2GHz with 32kb level 1 and 512kb level 2 cache memory, a VideoCore IV graphics processor, and is linked to a 1GB LPDDR2 memory module on the rear of the board.

✓ **GPIO**: A rather common feature of all the Raspberry, the Pi 3 features the same 40-pin general-purpose input-output (GPIO) header. This feature dates back to the Models; B+ and A+. So your existing GPIO will still function here with or without modifications. The slight difference here is the switch; UART is exposed on GPIO's pin, but that's handled internally by the operating system.

✓ **USB CHIP**: Nothing beyond the imagined and preexisting here. The same SMSC LAN9514 chip as its predecessor. 10/100 Ethernet connectivity and four USB channels to the board. As before, the SMSC chip connects to the SoC via as a single USB channel, acting as a USB-to-Ethernet adaptor and USB hub.

CHAPTER 4:
THE RASPBERRY Pi 3
SPECIFICATIONS

Here is a detailed specification of the Raspberry Pi 3:

- ➢ SoC: Broadcom BCM2837
- ➢ CPU: 4x ARM Cortex-A53, 1.2GHz
- ➢ GPU: Broadcom VideoCore IV
- ➢ RAM: 1GB LPDDR2
- ➢ Networking 10/100 Ethernet, 2.4GHz 802.11n wireless
- ➢ Bluetooth: Bluetooth 4 Classic, Bluetooth Low Energy
- ➢ Storage: MicroSD
- ➢ GPIO: 40-pin header, populated
- ➢ Ports: HDMI, 3.5mm analogue audio-video jack, 4xUSB, 2.0 Ethernet, Camera Serial Interface (CSI), Display Serial Interface (DSI)

CHAPTER 5:
BENCHMARK FOR THE RASPBERRY Pi 3

What is the point of having a new device if it doesn't significantly outshine the ones before it? Why waste cash on a device whose difference from the one you are using is its name? No point. But as regards the Raspberry Pi 3, the difference is not just great, it's a landmark, one that does not compare to the amount of money you use for purchasing it.

A series of test carried out by the company itself shows that the Raspberry Pi 3 promises to be more powerful than any Raspberry that had existed before it. Below are the categories and a series of test carried out on the all the Raspberry series:

1. Python GPIO (KHz) [The higher the better]

The Raspberry Pi's GPIO pins are the most commonly used with Python, but this leads to a CPU bottleneck. In this test, a simple RPi.GPIO program toggles a pin as rapidly as possible while a frequency counter measures how quickly it actually switches:

Model B+ clocked at 59.66

Model A+ clocked at 62.95

Zero clocked at 88.53

Pi 2 clocked at 197.2

Pi 3 clocked at 344.4

2. Whetstone (MWIPS) [The higher the better]

Developed by B.A. Wichman in the 1970s as a means of measuring a computer's speed, the Whetstone benchmark concentrates on floating-point performance. Despite its age, the benchmark offers a good insight into the peak floating-point performance of a processor:

Model B+ clocked at 232.558

Model A+ clocked at 236.858

Zero clocked at 340.498

Pi 2 clocked at 437.212

Pi 3 clocked at 711.363

3. Dhrystone (MIPS) [The higher the better]

Where Whetstone measures floating-point performance, Dhrystone was developed in the 1980s by Reinhold P Weicker to measure integer – or whole-number – performance. As with its floating-point equivalent, Dhrystone is still a useful synthetic benchmark for comparing different chips:

Model B+ clocked at 847.11

Model A+ clocked at 863.17

Zero clocked at 1237.29

Pi 2 clocked at 1671.58

Pi 3 clocked at 2458.1

4. Quake III Arena Timedemo [The higher the better]

The classic twitch shooter from industry pioneer id Software, Quake III Arena is heavily tied to the CPU performance of the Pi. The standard 'timedemo' was run at 1280×1024, high geometric, maximum texture detail, 32-bit texture quality, and trilinear filtering to obtain these results:

Model B+ clocked at 19.4

Model A+ clocked at 19.5

Zero clocked at 28.8

Pi 2 clocked at 57

Pi 3 clocked at 70.1

5. Power Draw [The lower the better]

You can't get extra performance without a few sacrifices. The Pi 3 draws the most power of the rest group, but its extra performance means it spends more time at idle. Those looking for maximum battery life should look at the Model A+ or the Pi Zero as an alternative:

Model B+ clocked at 0.25 when idle and 0.31 at load

Model A+ clocked at 0.11 when idle and 0.17 at load

Zero clocked at 0.1 when idle and 0.25 at load

Pi 2 clocked at 0.26 when idle and 0.42 at load

Pi 3 clocked at 0.31 when idle and 0.58 at load

6. SysBench (CPU) [The lower the better]

Offering support for multi-threaded operation – taking advantage of the four processing cores on the Pi 2 and Pi 3 – SysBench reveals just how far we've come since the original Raspberry Pi design. While single-threaded performance has improved greatly, the biggest gains go to multi-threaded programs.

Model B+ clocked at 510.81

Model A+ clocked at 502.42

Zero clocked at 349.43

Pi 2 clocked at 293.08 and 76.28 when multi-threaded

Pi 3 clocked at 182.225 and 49.02 when multi-threaded

The benchmark reveals to a great deal what to expect from the Raspberry Pi 3. The Pi 3 seems to clearly outshine the rest in almost all categories and stages except the "power draw" category. But as pointed out, the good comes with a little side effect. This particular one can be overlooked, but not ignored. The Raspberry creator would definitely work on improving this in newer series to come. It can only get better!

CHAPTER 6:
SETTING UP THE RASPBERRY Pi 3

New to the Raspberry experience? Don't worry, setting up is a walk in the park. The Raspberry Pi 3 may look puzzling to set up, but it's actually equally simple. The hardest part is loading the operating system onto the device. The Pi 3 doesn't have any inbuilt storage, but it uses a MicroSD card as a hard drive instead.

You can buy pre-prepared MicroSD cards from various Raspberry Pi 3 stock lists, with all the necessary software loaded and ready to go. If you want to use your own MicroSD card, however, you'll need to format it first, which can be done using inbuilt tools on both Windows and OSX.

Once you've got a formatted MicroSD Card, you'll need to prepare an operating system to load onto it. Due to the Pi 3's low-powered nature, it needs specially-adapted software based on popular Linux distros.

From the Raspberry Pi website, users can download the "New Out Of the Box Software" installer (NOOBS). Alongside an installation wizard and versions of operating systems like Ubuntu and OpenELEC, this package also contains a specially created version of Debian, called Raspbian.

Download NOOBS, extract the package's contents to your computer and transfer them to your formatted MicroSD card. Once that is done, insert the card into your Pi 3, plug in a monitor, keyboard, and mouse; connect the power and power it on.

Once it is turned on, the Pi 3 will automatically present you with a list of distros to choose from. Select one, and wait for it to install. Raspbian is recommended, as it's the one the Pi 3 is designed to work with best.

The Pi 3 will boot into the command line by default, but if you'd rather it boot to a more traditional desktop environment, this is easily fixed. After installation, a dialogue box will pop up - from here, you can change whether your Pi 3 boots into the command line or desktop.

Once that's done, you'll be all set to start using your Raspberry Pi 3 for whatever projects you like. Now, how simpler could this ever be?

Perhaps you prefer a step-by-step approach. What follows is a systematic order of putting your Raspberry Pi 3 together.

INSTALLING RASPBIAN

To get started installing Raspbian, visit Raspberry Pi Downloads and download the latest version. You will also need Win32 Disk Imager. With both downloaded, unzip Win32 Disk Imager and insert your card into the card reader.

Run the utility and select the correct drive letter (check in Windows Explorer) and click the file icon to browse to the directory where you have downloaded your latest Raspbian build.

To start the installation, click Write and wait. When the process is complete you will be notified.

Your Pi is ready to go!

USING RASPI-CONFIG

Once Raspbian is installed, you will be able to insert the SD card, power up your Pi, connect the HDMI cable (and a keyboard) and begin the process of configuring your new mini-computer. This is done with a utility called Raspi-config, which appears when you boot the Pi for the first time. You can change the options in this menu using your arrow keys, space bar, and Enter key.

The first thing you should do on your first launch of the Raspberry Pi is to run the Update. Make sure you have an Ethernet cable attached as the update will grab files from the Raspbian servers.

Raspi-config can be launched at any time from the command line with the command:

sudo raspi-config

CONTROLLING THE PI WITH SSH

Achieving "headless" use of your Raspberry Pi – using it without a dedicated monitor – is achievable using SSH.

As this is enabled by default, you don't even need to do anything with Raspi-config to set it up. As long as your Pi is connected to the same network as your computer and you have an SSH utility such as PuTTY, available from www.chiark.greenend.org.uk/~sgtatham/putty/download.html, running, you should be able to connect via SSH in seconds.

Configuring PuTTY is straightforward: In the Session screen, add the IP address of the Raspberry Pi in the Host Name (or IP address) field. Ensure SSH is selected and click Open. You can login to your Pi using the credentials provided by your chosen distro (for instance, if you use Raspbian, the username and password are displayed on the Raspbian download page).

OTHER DISTROS

Raspbian is the most popular choice for Raspberry Pi owners, but is by no means the only distro available for the computer.

You will also find:

- ✓ Debian "Wheezy": A slightly different build to the Raspbian - this is intended for use with Java.
- ✓ Arch Linux ARM: Based on Arch Linux, this distro boots in 10 seconds, but is unsuitable for most beginners.
- ✓ RISC OS: Available free of charge to Pi uses (RISC usually requires a license) this is the modern version of the British operating system developed in Cambridge and found on old Acorn computers.
- ✓ Moebius: A stripped-down operating system designed for projects requiring none of the bloat found on a standard OS.

ANDROID FOR RASPBERRY Pi 3

There is one other operating system available for the Pi. Unsurprisingly, it is the world's most popular ARM-based OS: Android!

While this allows the installation of many Android apps and games, the currently compatible version of the popular mobile OS is a couple of years behind. At present only Android 2.3 will run on the Pi.

Future development of Android for the Pi will hopefully bring Ice Cream Sandwich or Jelly Bean to the platform, but completion seems a long way off at present.

INSTALLING ANDROID ON YOUR RASPBERRY Pi 3

Installing Android onto the Pi is just as easy as installing Raspbian. Begin by downloading CyanogenMod 7.2, a custom Android ROM designed specifically for the Pi.

Once again, Win32 Disk Imager is required, so download and unzip, then run. With an SD card inserted into your card reader, select the correct device and browse for the Android ROM. Once selected, click Write to begin the installation.

As with Raspbian, when the installation of Android is complete, close the utility, safely eject the SD card and insert into your Raspberry Pi. Switch on and Android will be running!

CONFIGURING THE PI AS A MEDIA CENTER

Arguably the most popular use for a Pi is as a media center. Why splash out $$$ on a smart TV when you can get everything you need for under $40?

Thanks to the USB ports and networking, a Pi makes an excellent media device, both as a small set-top box streaming media from a larger PC or the web and as an all-in-one unit, accessing external hard disk drives and other storage media and outputting the media to your TV or sound system.

In order to do this, however, you will need to install a special version of XBMC known as Raspbmc.

INSTALLING XBMC ON THE RASPBERRY Pi 3

In order to turn your Pi into a media center, you will need to install Raspbmc, an alternative operating system for your Pi that's centered on the XBMC media player. After downloading the XBMC from the internet, it will need to be installed to SD using the same process used for installing Raspbian.

Ideally, you should use two SD cards, one for your Raspberry Pi's usual operating system and a second for XBMC. This way you can swap between roles as easily as switching the cards over, making the little computer even more flexible.

The following steps are explicitly for Windows users. Writing to the SD card on Linux and OS X requires command line access, although the process is virtually identical on each. Details on how to do this can be found on the OS X/Linux Installation guide at the Raspbmc website.

Installing Raspbmc for the Pi is as simple as installing the basic operating system. ·Begin by downloading the Raspbmc installer; once this is downloaded, connect an empty, formatted SD card into your reader before unzipping and running installer.exe.

Your SD card should be detected. Check the box against it and select Install, then wait. When the process is complete you will be informed, at which point you should close the installer utility, carefully remove the SD card and insert it into your Pi.

With the Ethernet cable connected, switch on the Pi. The device will connect to the Internet to download further data, and once complete it will boot into the Raspberry Pi port of XBMC – your pocket-sized media center is ready!

PRINCIPLES OF RUNNING XBMC ON A RASPBERRY PI

Although setting up XBMC and getting started for viewing videos and enjoying music on the Pi is relatively easy, using the Pi as a media center is a little different to the usual setup. Unless you're using an extremely large capacity SD card (SDHC with a maximum of 32 GB is the recommended format, although some types of SDXC are believed to work) you will need to run media from an external hard disk drive, a USB storage device or an external optical drive. XBMC offers various streaming options thanks to its wide selection of add-ons, of course... it all really depends on your preferred media choices. You should also consider a powered USB hub if you're planning on maxing out your existing expansion options.

A network attached storage box might be one solution for media stored on HDD, or you might rely on sharing content across your home network from a PC in your office, bedroom or den.

One thing to be aware of is that Netflix will not run on the Raspberry Pi (at the time of writing) due to its reliance on Microsoft's Silverlight. This is something that Netflix hasn't yet commented on, and with around one million Pi devices sold by early 2013, it seems unlikely that this will be the case long-term.

A final point on using the Pi as a media center: This is one feature where you will really find that the device gets some wear and tear, so make sure you have a versatile and hardy case for the computer!

EXTENDING XBMC

Installing Raspbmc is only the first step in setting up your media center. A variety of add-ons enables you to extend this software considerably, many of which we've covered earlier. For instance, you can watch the news online using XBMC, add podcast feeds to XBMC and enjoy YouTube videos on XBMC. Additionally, you can re-skin the interface using free XMBC themes, and even watch Hulu – not to mention enjoying free cable and sports channels piped directly to your TV from the Internet!

CHAPTER 7:
PROGRAMMING THE RASPBERRY
Pi 3

One of the key reasons for the development of the Pi was to create an affordable computer that children and students could use as a platform for application development. Programming on the Pi is made simple by the provision of various tools bundled in with the Raspbian operating system. With the emergence of the Raspberry Pi 3, programming is much easier, you now have available a 64bit operating system.

Whether you're happy learning to program applications with Python or you prefer one of the alternatives that can be installed, you'll need a plan or an outline for your application, plenty of time to spend getting it right and some basic background in coding.

THE PYTHON

The primary programming language provided with the Pi is Python. If you have experience with this language, then you should be able to start coding straight away.

Of course, if you're 7, the chances are that you haven't had the time to get to grips with Python. Fortunately, the Raspberry Pi ships with a useful Python module called **Pygame**, essentially a game construction kit that should enable you to have fun and learn basic game building principles at the same time. There are also several programs included that have been written in Python; these programs are included, so you can get an idea of what can be achieved.

Note also that Python is a cross-platform scripting language, which means that you can program on a Windows computer or a Mac, save the project and then run it on your Pi.

THE MULTI-PURPOSE RASPBERRY

Although Python is considered the core programming tool for young users of the Pi, other languages can also be used:

- ✓ Java has been tested, although the resulting program may not run until Oracle releases the JVM for the Pi, expected sometime in 2013.
- ✓ PHP can also be successfully used, opening up some interesting possibilities for using this mini-computer as a web server.
- ✓ Scratch is included in the Raspbian distro, an easy to use development tool aimed at children with a drag-and-drop GUI that makes building conditions and in-game situations extremely simple. Scratch is developed by MIT Media Lab and Life-long Kindergarten Group.

Projects using the GalaxC, Lazarus, and Groovy languages can all be compiled and tested on a Pi.

CHAPTER 8:
PRODUCTIVITY REDEFINED WITH THE RASPBERRY Pi 3

The Raspberry series were indeed beauties in the technological sense. These chips contributed immensely to the construction of robots and other machines. Coding got simpler and easier. The shape of the chip made it fit in effortlessly into any construction. The fact it is easily programmable made it even friendlier. In all sense, the Raspberry series were "pocket-friendly".

However, with the emergence of the Raspberry Pi 3, comes more! More fun, more comfort, more productivity.

Here are some the things you can do with the new Raspberry Pi 3:

1. BUILD A WIRELESS SENSOR NETWORK

I am sure we would recall that the Raspberry Pi 3's Broadcom BCM43438 radio chip is high-performance yet low-power, thus, a perfect tool for building ones' one sensor networks. From cameras to temperature sensors, all can be connected to the Pi 3 and they connect via the wireless LAN enabling for quick and easy Internet of Things (IoT). One can even go a step further to drop the "powerdraw" further and build a Bluetooth Low Energy network with multiple Pi 3 systems. For remote installations, try pairing to a cheap mobile handset via Bluetooth Classic.

2. STREAM AUDIO VIA BLUETOOTH

As well as wireless 802.11n and Bluetooth Low Energy, the BCM43438 chip supports Bluetooth Classic mode, including the Advanced Audio Distribution Profile (A2DP). Support for A2DP means it's possible to configure a Pi 3 as a streamer, either receiving audio from a device such as a smartphone or a tablet for amplification via HDMI or analogue outputs, or sending its own audio to a remote A2DP destination such as a Bluetooth enabled sound bar or hi-fi system. You can even build on existing Pi-powered Bluetooth projects without having to buy a USB radio dongle.

3. GAMING AT THE NEXT LEVEL

oThe Raspberry Pi 3 in the world of gaming has also gone a step further in redefining that sphere. The Raspberry Pi has always had a powerful graphics processor, and now that the central processor can keep up, we're going to see increasingly complex games being built on the system. For those who enjoy the classics, the Pi 3's increased performance means smoother emulation in general, plus support for emulating newer or more demanding systems and titles. For others, there's promise that future Pi games will be able to give mainstream titles a real run for their money in the graphics department. This automatically translates that the Raspberry Pi 3 should withstand everything and anything we throw at it. But never throw GTA V at it nor Battlefield 4, the Raspberry to handle those are still in embryo.

4. BUILD A THIN CLIENT INFRASTRUCTURE

We've seen the Raspberry Pi used to build a pseudo thin client infrastructure in the past, but the need for local storage in the form of the MicroSD card has kept it from being a truly thin implementation. The promised support for PXE network boot means that a Pi 3, unlike any other model, can be used as a thin client without the need for any local storage, decreasing deployment cost and increasing reliability – and no more risk of anyone walking off with the SD card!

5. RUN 64-BIT CODE

The Raspberry Pi 3 not only caters for the desperate gamer, but also for the inquisitive coder. How? The BCM2837 at the heart of the Pi 3 uses the 64-bit ARMv8 microarchitecture – this can be compared to the 32-bit ARMv7 and ARMv6 of previous models. As well as widening compatibility for running other operating systems, the shift to 64-bit holds the potential to improve performance - but it's going to be up to the community to demonstrate that splitting Raspbian into 32-bit and 64-bit variants offer advantages enough to outweigh the headache of maintaining and supporting two distinct operating system builds.

NO LIMITS WITH THE RASPBERRY Pi 3

While running a Raspberry Pi 3 as a media center seems to be an extremely popular option, it isn't the only way in which this little computer can be put to work. There are various ways in which the Pi 3 can be used to achieve various purposes and to complete many different tasks, from using it as a NAS to running a web server or even a computer.

Away from the five most widely held things that can be handled by the Pi 3 as mentioned earlier, there exist still across the web, dimensions, and platform in which the Raspberry Pi 3 can be used.

7. RASPBERRY AS KINDLE READER

One of the most remarkable hacks for a Pi is to couple it up to a Kindle e-reader, using the latter as an e-ink display for the former. The connection is via a USB to MicroUSB cable and requires that you jailbreak the kindle, install a terminal emulator and a tool called USB Network. Once the Kindle has been unlocked and the necessary utilities installed, you will be on the way to using the e-reader as a display for your Pi 3. Note that this can only be done with the Kindle models that are equipped with an integrated keyboard.

8. RASPBERRY AS A NAS BOX

With the amazing features that the Raspberry pi 3 possess, one cannot limit its possibilities. Aside its possible configuration as a media center, another is saving your media files to your Raspbian device with a NAS box; a very easy to setup project (assuming you have an existing Raspberry Pi). Although it may be suitable for streaming HD videos, a Pi 3 NAS box can be set up as a low-power NAS.

In other to complete this project, you will need:

- ✓ Raspberry Pi 3
- ✓ An SD card configured with the bootable OS
- ✓ A USB connected hard disk drive
- ✓ Ethernet cable for connection to your network

You will also need to configure the Samba server on your Pi (running one of the debian distros) and the Samba client on your windows, Linx, Mac or Andriod device.

9. RASPBERRY AS A "CARPUTER"

End your TV nostalgia dreams of being David Hasselhoff driving a black Trans-am in Knight Rider – with a Raspberry Pi you can set up your own "carputer" (although it may not be too hot on conversation).

Building a Pi "carputer" is a bit of a tricky one, although it has been achieved by several users. The key component is a touchscreen display, enabling you to interact with the chosen software (typically Raspbmc as it includes a live weather service) but you'll also need to deal with powering both devices, mounting the display and potentially incorporating a 3G widget for media streaming.

"Pursuit mode" not included, sadly.

10. THE WIRELESS RASPBERRY Pi 3 RADIO

This is perhaps the biggest feature on the Raspberry Pi 3, and the most talked about. In fact, it is the reason why the Pi 3 is ranked over all other predecessors. Its on-board wireless LAN connectivity allows users to connect to a wireless network without trying up a USB port.

All you need for the wireless setup is these:

- ✓ Raspberry Pi 3
- ✓ 2.4GHz 802.11b/g/n wireless network
- ✓ Your network name (SSID)
- ✓ Your network key (PSK)

The inclusion of a Broadcom BCM43438 radio chip on the Raspberry Pi 3 means it is the first model to offer built-in wireless networking. For anyone who has used a USB wireless dongle with a Pi before, the configuration will be straightforward; for everyone else, here's how you hook your Pi 3 up to your wireless network: The Raspberry Pi 3's on-board wireless radio has drivers' pre-installed in the latest version of Raspbian, but if you're upgrading from an older installation, you'll need to install them manually. Connect the Pi to a wired network, open a terminal, and type the following:

sudo apt-get update sudo apt-get dist-upgrade

Reboot to apply the changes.

CONNECTING FROM THE DESKTOP

The easiest way to connect to a wireless network is through the desktop. The network icon can be found at the top-right of the screen, near the system clock. If you have a wired Ethernet cable connected, disconnect it now. Click the icon to view a list of wireless networks within range. Find the network matching your network name (known as the SID), then click on it to begin connecting. If your network doesn't appear, it may be out of range; try moving the Pi and the access point or router closer together and try again.

If your network is encrypted with WEP or WPA, you'll be prompted for the network key, also known as the pre-shared key or PSK. If you're not sure what this is, it's usually written on the underside of your access point or router, or on a card attached to the back. Type this in carefully, making sure it matches, and click the OK button. The network icon will change into a wireless symbol, which fills up blue as it tries to connect. If the connection is successful, it will stabilize and display the current signal strength; if not, make sure you chose the right network name and entered the correct key.

CONNECTING FROM THE COMMAND LINE

If you are using the lite version of Raspbian, without the desktop, you'll need to configure your wireless network at the command line instead. At the console, type the following command:

sudo nano /etc/wpa_supplicant/wpa_supplicant.conf

Scroll to the bottom of the file, and enter a network definition using the following template:

network={ssid="NetworkName"psk="NetworkKey"key_mgmt=WPA-PSK}

...where Network Name is your network's SSID and Network Key is the encryption key. If you are connecting to a WEP rather than WPA/WPA2 network, put **key_mgmt=NONE**. If you are connecting to an open network, you only need the SSID.

Save the file with CTRL+O, then exit with CTRL+X. In a few seconds, your Pi should connect.

11. RASPBERRY AS INTERNET RADIO

Rather than using your Raspberry Pi as an all-in-one media center, you might prefer to limit its abilities to playing back music streamed from the Internet.

There are different approaches to this as a Pi Internet radio can be setup without a GUI. In most cases, this is preferable (for obvious reasons of space), and the software used can be accessed via SSH.

12. SECURITY SYSTEM

Do you want to know what is going on in a particular room of your house or outside your property? If so, you can use your Pi as a security system, using webcams to observe and a network connection to view from another computer or even from an entirely different location.

There are several varying descriptions on how to achieve this available on the web, but the most important aspects are to use webcams that have Linux drivers and to use either powered USB cables or a powered USB hub in order to run the cameras. This project is heavy on USB, and as the Ethernet port on the Raspberry Pi is also part of the onboard USB, you can see where there might be some drain on available power.

13. BABYCAM SERVER

Working to a similar principle (but with added microphones) you can also use your Pi to manage a babycam server, enabling you to observe and listen to activity coming from your little ones.

Depending on which approach you use, however, this can be a tough nut to crack, due to the problems with compression, the results of night photography and the delay (up to 10 seconds for the image to be captured, compressed and routed to your viewing device).

14. HOME AUTOMATION SERVER

If you've ever seen a sci-fi film in which the heating, lighting, security and entertainment in a home are all controlled from the same remote device and thought "I want some of that!" then this is the Raspberry Pi project for you.

It is also – if you're coming to the concept fresh – by far the most expensive, as it involves introducing new hardware around your home, enabling you to interact fully through a remote (typically a smartphone) via your Pi.

15. TEST OF LIVE WEB SERVER

Hosting a website can prove expensive, particularly if all you need to share with the web is a single "about" page that perhaps links to other online locations. Paying several dollars a month for this is bad economics, so you might consider taking advantage of your Raspberry Pi to host your online presence.

Thanks to LAMP and SSH this is made possible, even enabling you to run a database-driven website!

PenguinTutor explains how you can setup your Pi as your own personal web server for personal use or for sharing with the web. Note that for the latter, you will require a static IP address.

16. WIRELESS ACCESS POINT

Finally, you can use your Raspberry Pi as a Wireless Access Point, extending the range of your router. This can have a range of benefits, all of which can be implemented using Pi-Point.

With your Pi setup as a Wireless Access Point, the device can be used both as a wireless extender and as a secondary router for offering free wireless access to the surrounding area. This, in turn, will help you to learn more about wireless networking and security.

CHAPTER 9:
THE RASPBERRY AS A
MINICOMPUTER

The idea of describing the Raspberry Pi 3 as a minicomputer seems "overblown" to certain people, but then, how can one possibly describe a micro credit card shaped board capable of programming and functioning as an operating system?

The Raspberry Pi 3 has a whole host of different applications, including as a mini-PC. It's not hugely powerful, but it's capable of doing basic word processing and office tasks, and also works well for simple internet browsing, although HTML-intensive pages might slow it down.

It's also been used extensively for retro gaming and emulation - it's just about powerful enough to run classic NES and SNES games, and the newly-announced OpenGL support means it could potentially handle from as recent as the early 2000s.

IoT projects are popular amongst the Pi's vibrant modding community, and users have turned their Pis into weather monitoring stations, home automation controllers, smart mirrors and more.

The Raspberry Pi is also perfect for use as a thin client for businesses with remote access needs. There's software to support Microsoft Remote Desktop, VMWare, X3270 and Citrix.

So you've got your cables, your SD card, your distro of choice and you've been using your Raspberry Pi as a mini computer, perhaps housed in a small case. There's more that you can do, however. The Pi is graced with a very useful pair of pin-based connectors, allowing for the addition of further functions and components. Thanks to breakout boards you can turn your Pi into a programmable Arduino-esque device, completely spinning the concept of this little computer on its head. Beyond breakout boards, you will find even more fascinating tools and components that can be added to a Pi.

You can take your Raspberry Pi to the next level by taking advantage of a breakout board. Using the GPIO, I2C and SPI pins, these boards come in pre-assembled or kit form, enabling you to extend the functionality of your device. The idea is that you are able to build upon the hardware of the Raspberry Pi by adding more integrated components.

These boards can be used to power other equipment, such as lights, radios or even model train sets. Breakout boards can be purchased online from sellers such as:

➢ Hobbytronics
➢ ModMyPi
➢ Adafruit

You'll also find sellers on Amazon and eBay offering expansions to the Pi.

As you've probably guessed, some understanding of electronics is required before you connect a breakout board.

CHAPTER 10:
TRICKS AND TWEAKS OF THE
RASPBERRY Pi 3

Perhaps it is your thing, to always want to fully utilize every device that you possess and you are wondering if the Raspberry Pi 3 can achieve that similar goal, wonder no more! We have made a duty to unveil some tricks, tips, and tweaks of the Raspberry, which can ensure full utilization of the device if followed to the letter.

Whether you're planning on setting up a media center, turning your Pi into a NAS box or simply using it for its core purpose to learn programming, it should be extremely clear just how versatile this little box of tricks really is.

Installation is a cinch, software is easy to install, and the entire setup will cost you under $50. That's a pretty good deal, especially when you consider that the more recent 512 MB models were made available without a price increase.

Indeed, it is easy to see why this little box of wonders has shipped 1 million units!

You now know everything you need to get started with your Raspberry Pi – so here are ten tips for successful use.

- ✓ Safely boot your Pi computer by ensuring that the SD card is inserted before switching on.
- ✓ Launch the GUI by typing startX from the command line.
- ✓ Access the Raspberry Pi via SSH from a desktop computer using software such as PuTTY.
- ✓ Make sure you have a good case for the RaspPi, one that offers ventilation and protection.
- ✓ Various distros (including Debian and Android) are available for the Raspberry Pi. You could run them all, installing them on separate SD cards in order to gain the most flexibility from your mini-computer.
- ✓ Your Pi is particularly suited to running as a media center thanks to the Raspbmc distro.
- ✓ Originally intended as a device to teach children how to program, a good selection of coding tools are available for the Raspberry Pi.
- ✓ There are many uses for this computer, a hugely flexible piece of equipment. Don't forget, however, that it can also run the word-processing software, email clients, and web browsers.
- ✓ You can extend the possibilities of the Pi by adding breakout boards.

Safely shut down your Pi by switching to the command line and typing:

sudo shutdown (sudo shutdown -r to reset).

Remember to remove the power cable when the computer is shut down.

More so, there other tips and tricks of the Raspberry Pi 3 which we intend to unveil. They include:

HOW TO TRANSFER YOUR MICROSD CARD

The best way to use your new Raspberry Pi 3 is with a fresh Raspbian or NOOBS installation. To use an existing Raspbian MicroSD card with the Pi 3, you'll need to make a modification. In your older Pi, boot Raspbian and open a terminal. Type the following command:

sudo apt-get update sudo apt-get dist-upgrade

Shut the Pi down: *sudo shutdown –h*

Now transfer your MicroSD card to your Pi 3 and your existing operating system will boot. Finally, make sure you're up to date:

sudo apt-get update sudo apt-get upgrade

ENABLING OPENGL ACCELERATION

Available exclusively on the Raspberry Pi 2 and 3 thanks to their increased RAM, OpenGL 3D acceleration support is currently in the experimental stage. You can enable the new driver with the following command:

sudo apt-get update && sudo apt-get install xcompmgr libgl1-mesa-driBe

Warned though: With the OpenGL driver installed, you'll no longer be able to swap your MicroSD card between the Pi 2 or Pi 3 and any other model, as it will fail to boot on any Raspberry Pi with less than 1GB of RAM.

USE THE 2.4GHZ BAND

The BCM43438 has a single-band wireless radio. You need to be running a 2.4GHzonly or dual-band 2.4/5GHz network to successfully connect.

PROGRAMMING FOR THE RASPBERRY PI 3

If you're writing new software for the Raspberry Pi, or porting existing software ICKS across, there are a few tricks that will help you get the most out of the Raspberry Pi 3...

Write multi-threaded applications

Where you can, make your software multi-threaded. The Pi 2 and Pi 3 both feature quad-core processors and a fully threaded application will run up to four times faster than one which runs in a single thread. In scenarios where true multithreading isn't possible, look at spawning multiple copies of your program and splitting the workload between them.

Use NEON extensions

ARM's NEON single instruction multiple-data (SIMD) extensions are fully supported on the BCM2836 and BCM2837 chips used in the Pi 2 and 3, and using them offers an impressive speed boost: switching from the standard LINPAC benchmark on the Pi 3 to a version compiled with NEON support boosts its score from 193MFLOPs to 459MFLOPs. NEON applications, however, won't run on the BCM2835 used on the B+, A+, and Zero.

INVESTIGATE 64-BIT SUPPORT

At present, the 64-bit Cortex-A53 cores on the Raspberry Pi 3 are used exclusively in 32-bit mode. If you're looking to port a new operating system to the Pi 3, consider doing so as a native 64-bit version; if you can prove that doing so offers a performance advantage, we may see an official 64-bit Raspbian build released in the future.

BLUETOOTH SUPPORT

At the time of writing, the driver for Bluetooth Classic and Bluetooth Low Energy modes has not yet been finalized. By the time you read this, however, you should be able to install the modules after the aforementioned *apt-get dist-upgrade* using: *sudo apt-get install pi-bluetooth*

CHAPTER 11:
THE FUTURE OF THE RASPBERRY

As we continue to experience the Raspberries in different dimensions, with the Pi 3 coming as a shocker, we can no longer limit our idea of what the next Raspberry tends to unfold. Anything can happen; I must say. The future of the Raspberry is positive and perhaps immeasurable starting with the Raspberry Pi 3 itself. In a recent interview with the director of Hardware Engineering for the Raspberry Foundation; James Adams, when asked about the "hypothetical" Raspberry Pi 4, and what to expect, he said, "I'd like to see USB 3.0 added, as it really is the universal solution for adding peripherals–especially higher bandwidth ones like disk drives, network interfaces – and removes the requirement for things like SATA."

This rather "blurred" comment, opens the mind of the inquisitive still into the many possibilities of what to expect from the Raspberry in the future. Away from the future, in the present, the Raspberry Pi 3 continues to wow the world at large. Inventors are consciously including the Raspberry Pi 3 into their inventions - an act that was the core reason why the originators created the Raspberry in the first instance – for learning and programming.

Recently, there were confirmed news that the Raspberry Pi is set to be used as the brain of an autonomous racing car. The idea comes from Piborg, which makes robotic kits for the tiny computer. It has built a track at its UK headquarters and plans a racing series called Formula Pi using the self-driving vehicles. PiBorg has set up a Kickstarter campaign with a modest £2500 goal.

Formula Pi gives developers a chance to hack about with autonomous driving code that they can download from the Formula Pi site. The code can be modified and then cars can race other Raspberry Pi-based cars on a special track.

Entrants can sign up for the race for £35 and receive a customizable lid that holds the Raspberry Pi computer on a racing car. The aim of the contest is to go as fast as possible around the track while avoiding other cars. The track features laser controlled finishing line and the car will run on the Zeroborg motor platform.

Raspberry Fi foundation's founder, Eben Upton, made comments that "rumours" of Android support for the microcomputer are "promising".

Android support for Raspberry Pi 3 has been rumoured after Google opened a new tree for the microcomputer in its Android Open Source Project repository in April.

He said this month, upon being made a CBE in the Queen's Birthday List: "It's a promising sign and a nice compliment to the open source community." But he added that the foundation has not had time to work on developing support, because it is focused on building as many devices as possible, though many open source Android users would be keen to make use of the operating system on a Raspberry Pi 3.

Heard of Kodi? Kodi has revealed a Raspberry Pi 3 case, its first hardware release, to turn the Raspberry Pi 3 and other members of the Pi series into a budget media center, reports The Verge.

Created in partnership with Flirc, the aluminium case has been designed to look attractive plus act as a heat sink to keep the Pi cool inside. It is currently available as a limited edition, but high demand could convince Kodi to make more.

A percentage of the profits will be donated to cancer research.

The £4 Raspberry Pi Zero has received a boost in functionality, with the announcement of a new onboard camera connector. The FPC connector is the same part that graces the foundation's compute module, used in development and industrial environments. The Raspberry Pi Foundation's engineers were able to fit the component onto the minuscule board's right-hand side by reshuffling the existing elements, without increasing the original unit's size.

The announcement follows the launch of two Sony-made 8 megapixel imaging modules last month, which allow users to capture fixed-focus images at a 3280 x 2464 resolution.

The new feature was added during the production hiatus directly following the Zero's launch, founder Eben Upton explained, after the foundation's entire stock ran out in a matter of hours.

The foundation has apparently learned its lesson from the original Zero's launch, and there will be 30,000 of the newly updated models available today.

Upton also assured that the foundation will "be making thousands more each day until demand is met".

Ubuntu Mate for the Raspberry Pi now features support for the Raspberry Pi 3's new built-in WiFi and Bluetooth chips.

The open-source operating system, a specialized variant of one of the most popular Linux builds, has now been updated to the second Beta version of build 16.04.

The OS now has a new welcome screen, and several features unique to the Raspberry Pi. It also features support for hardware-accelerated OpenGL, a display rendering technology that allows for far more sophisticated graphics processing.

Martin Wimpress, the leader of the volunteer team responsible for overseeing the project, made a point of specifically thanking Pi Podcast presenters Joe Ressington, Winkle ink and Isaac Carter for testing the build.

According to Wimpress, the three gave "valuable feedback", saying that "thanks to them this Beta is in a pretty decent shape".

The Beta is available to download now for the Raspberry Pi 2 and Raspberry Pi 3.

It is paramount to stress that the vision behind the Raspberry creation is to enable children and teenager learn the core of programming, as released by the Raspberry foundation. Away from these, the Raspberry is well equipped to meet the basic needs of a programmer and a regular system user. From sound box to a coding tool, the Raspberry meets every need.

Across the globe, we continue to witness the many ways the Raspberry has been used to produce and generate new tools and devices that makes life more fun and entertaining. From gaming to cameras to sensor to drivers for driverless cars, the future of the Raspberry is promising.

Recently, the news reports of a digital girl for the year 2015, Yasmin Bey, who through the aid of the Raspberry Pi went pro in computing and won an award for doing just that. You too might be the next pro. Wouldn't you rather join the league of Raspberry users across the world and unleash the genius inside you? If you are a parent, get one for your kids. You will discover that it was, after all, the best gift you can offer a kid of this age. Thank us later.

Even at age 15, she's already experienced enough with computing to know it is what she loves, and her efforts have been rewarded by winning the prestigious Digital Girl of the Year award for 2015.

"It was really, really cool. So cool," Yasmin says of winning the award. "When I heard how many people applied for it − I think it was in the 30,000s − I was amazed. If you do the math and figure out your chance of actually winning, [the odds] are rather substantial." Entry was via video where applicants had to answer questions.

But then, what exactly did Yasmin do? She built a robot using the Raspberry Pi - again, another possibility with the Raspberry. She used the Pi 2, and now we have within our reach, something more powerful, the Raspberry Pi 3.

As well as winning Digital Girl of the Year, Yasmin has been nominated for the 2016 FDM everywoman in Technology Awards. These awards are for women who are role models in the tech sector, showing that women work in STEM industries too, as a way to inspire young girls and women to keep on with STEM subjects if they want to. Yasmin is a finalist for the "One To Watch" award, among other school and university students. Clearly, the rest of the world is beginning to take notice of Yasmin and her abilities. We still look forward to more inventions from Yasmin, and of course, you, as soon as you put your Raspberry Pi 3 to uttermost use.

More so, you'll find through regular use of your Pi 3 that many other cables and components can be used, in addition to those aforementioned:

- ✓ Cables – you may want to take advantage of the Pi's audio out port and connect the computer to your surround sound system. Alternatively, you might like to output video to a device other than a HDMI monitor – something you can only do with an RCA cable.
- ✓ Cooling components – if you're planning on a lot of HD decoding on your Raspberry Pi 3, you will need to consider some form of cooling. While a decent case will provide vent slots above the main CPU, you should perhaps also consider some form of heat sink. There are several available, from the small, traditional radiators found in desktop PCs to the more unique, "wavy metal" variety.
- ✓ Wi-Fi – the Pi will support a large number of USB wireless dongles. You'll need to do some research to find the full list of compatible devices, but you shouldn't need to spend too much to find one that is both suitable and easy to set up.
- ✓ A hook-and-loop fastener strip such as Velcro – if you're planning to deploy your Raspberry Pi as a media center, NAS box or simply as a computer for development (as intended!), you might consider some means of attaching it to your table, back of your TV or atop your hard disk drives. Unlike a desktop computer whose weight dominates over

movement from the cables, a Pi will often be pushed about, particularly by an Ethernet cable. Using a strip of something like Velcro will put an end to this, fixing the computer in place and avoiding potentially nasty knocks.